GW01312069

The Sheffield Arms c1910. A painting by Ernest Marillier from
'The Wonderful Weald' by Arthur Beckett, published 1911.

THE SHEFFIELD ARMS
The Life of a 200-year-old Sussex Coaching Inn
HOME OF TRADING BOUNDARIES

Angela Wigglesworth

Published by New Generation Publishing in 2021

Copyright © Angela Wigglesworth 2021

Design: Andy Gammon Art and Design, Lewes

First Edition

ISBN: 978-1-80031-311-8

www.newgeneration-publishing.com

New Generation Publishing

Books by the same author

Falkland People (*Peter Owen*)

People of Scilly (*Sutton*)

People of Wight (*Sutton*)

Lewes, a Photographic History of your Town (*Frith Publications*)

The Chair Man (*New Generation Publishing*)

Not Just Another Swan (*New Generation Publishing*)

Dedicated to the memory of Roy Lingham
(1922 to 2021)
A kind and gentle man

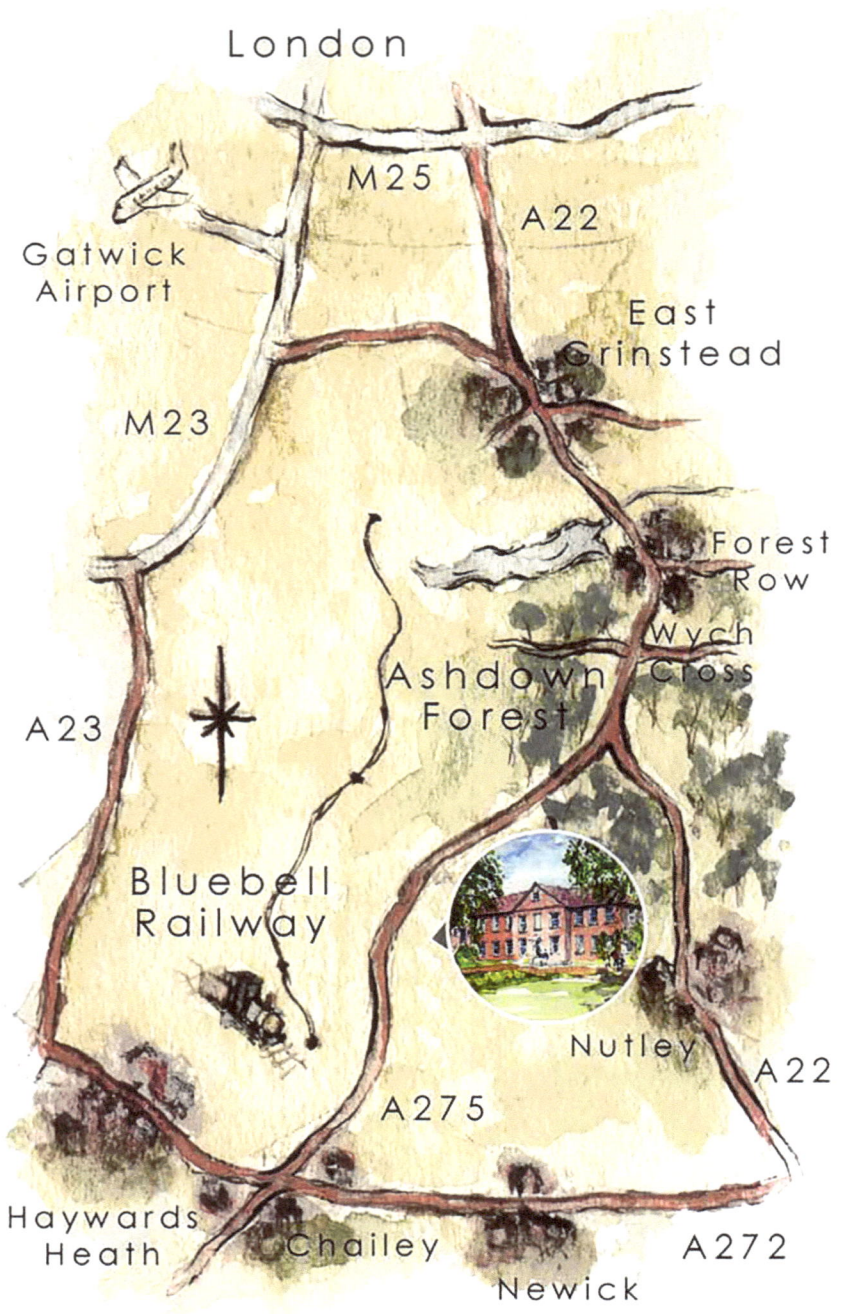

London

M25

A22

Gatwick
Airport

East
Grinstead

M23

Forest
Row

Wych
Cross

A23

Ashdown
Forest

Bluebell
Railway

Nutley

A22

A275

**Map showing the
Sheffield Arms**
*by kind permission of
Trading Boundaries*

Haywards
Heath

Chailey

A272

Newick

Brighton

CONTENTS

First Lord Sheffield
(1735-1821)

EARLY YEARS

John Baker Holroyd was born in 1735 and came from a Yorkshire family that had moved to Ireland. A soldier and Member of Parliament, he became the first Earl of Sheffield in 1768 and two years later he bought the Sheffield Park estate in Sussex from Earl de la Warr for £30,900. James Wyatt, a well-known architect of the time, was commissioned to redesign the house and Capability Brown to create pleasure grounds around it.

Seven years later Holroyd decided to build a coaching inn on the London to Brighton road on land he owned at Sheffield Green near his Sheffield Park home. Before that time the route of the old London to Brighton road had run via Godstone, Uckfield and Lewes but in the 1770s a more direct route had been made across Sheffield Green, by-passing Uckfield, with a turnpike road (where tolls are collected) from Godstone to Lewes and a toll house at the top of The Green. But there was no stage (stopping place) between East Grinstead and Lewes. Sheffield Green was equidistant from both. 'This road,' Holroyd noted, 'was the shortest and best road by upwards of two miles to Lewes.'

With the rising popularity of Brighton, what better place to have an inn?

'When a good inn is established,' he wrote, 'a great deal of company will pass this way to Brighthelmstone (Brighton) – many do now notwithstanding the want of a proper stage'. He lists the assets of an inn at Sheffield Green: there would be business from the house & visitors' servants and horses; Justices of the Peace; post bag; persons to see Sheffield Park; people on business; stagecoaches to breakfast or dine.'

Before this time a landed proprietor might have provided accommodation for the family and servants, his steward, bailiff and agricultural labourers, his guests, their servants and horses, visitors on business. But by the 1770s much had changed, and only immediate house servants would be accommodated in the mansion and only the more genteel visitors would expect to stay with their host overnight. Justices increasingly conducted business sitting in pairs rather than alone and for that neutral territory was essential. The erection of a major inn within easy reach of Holroyd's new mansion could be a great convenience to his house and way of life.

Building began in 1777. Stone for the foundation came from Chelwood Common; 100,000 bricks from Trickland kiln; tiles from kilns in South Chailey and Ditchling; lime was brought in and 197 loads of sand were dug by William Feldwick. Other local workmen paid for their labour included John Botting, carpenter; Thomas Hill for firestone from Godstone, including carriage of the same; Daniel Warnett for paving stones and for a man who looked after the inn on Sundays; Thomas Water for hair and tan; James Fuller for cleaning twenty-four windows on April 12, 1779, (just before the inn's opening?); George Bowring, plumber; John Billingshurst, brickmaker; Richard Tamplin for nails and screws. In 1779, a last-minute request came from Daniel Warnett (the builder) who sent in a bill for a milestone (necessary publicity) and a mounting block.

In a memorandum dated 1777 Holroyd describes his plans: 'there will be three garrets over the centre of the house. The bar looks out over the turnpike road, the entrance, the tap room & the kitchen and the cellar door. There is a cellar under the large parlour 23 ft by 18 and a wine cellar under the staircase and passage. There will be lofts over the whole of the stables. At one end there will be a granary and the other good room for stable people.'

The shell of the building was erected between March 1777 and January 1778 at an approximate cost of £470, not including bricks made at the Trickland kiln. The accounts and many of the supporting vouchers survive although there are none for finishing

Early 19th century Sheffield Arms sign with additional later notices.
Photo: by kind permission of Roy Lingham

Unique Milestone & The Sheffield Arms, near Danehill & Fletching, Sussex.

The original milestone built in 1779 with the Sheffield Arms in the background.

the building which was perhaps done by the first tenant.
Lord Sheffield's initials J B H (John Baker Holroyd) 1777, are
inscribed on a stone at the back of the building and can still be seen
today.

When the inn opened in 1779 and the first horse-drawn mail
coaches made it a regular stopping place on their journey from
London to Brighton, it was known as the Lewes Arms, then renamed
the New Inn, until in 1787 Lord Sheffield decided it should be called
the Sheffield Arms. It was, as he had planned, used by visiting
Justices of the Peace, businessmen, Sheffield Place guests and staff,
breakfast and dinner for stagecoach travellers, and a change of
horses.

The first tenant was John Fletcher who came on March 25 and took
over the lease which included the neighbouring farms of Vigoes,
Gobels and Trickland at an annual rent of £71. But two years later he
was in debt and surrendered the lease to Edward Hook for £60.
Fletcher's goods were sold to pay off the rent – the Sheffield Park
estate bought a post-chaise, goods in the stable and two servants'
beds over it, a copper furnace, a mash-tub and stand in the wash
house, a cooler, five tubs and a furnace in the brew house. The sale
made £321.15s.7d, just enough to pay his debt of £294.18s but with
little left over.

By 1782 Hook, too, was in debt and the following year a licence was
granted to the estate steward, Jethro Turner, who held it for eight
years. It seems it was difficult to find another tenant despite
persuasive publicity stating what a convenient stop it was on the
London to Brighton route, how it was elegantly fitted up and that
there were 80 acres of land included in the price. By 1789 the offer
had increased to include 224 acres of land.

It took 15 years to find another tenant. He was James Elliot but he
stayed no longer than a year. In fact, not many tenants stayed more

Window bill advertising the first cricket match to be played at Sheffield Park in 1845, catered for by Sheffield Arms landlord, James Comber.
Photo courtesy Mrs.H.Rawlings

than a few years. But there were exceptions. The Comber family (James and John) were there from 1844 to 1871 and catered for many of the Sheffield Park cricket matches. An early poster advertising the first match shows it was to be played 'with eleven gentlemen from Fletching and Newick, eleven gentlemen from Chailey and Newick' and that 'A cold collation will be provided on the Ground by the Public's obedient Servant, James Comber, Sheffield Arms Inn, Fletching.' The date was August 28, 1845, a year after James Comber had arrived at the inn.

It was under his tenancy that the Sheffield Arms hosted one of its most prestigious events. On January 18th, 1853, the third Lord Sheffield, then known as Viscount Pevensey, celebrated his 21st birthday there. Roger Packham in his book, Cricket in the Park, describes the scene as it appeared in the Illustrated London News of that year:

About five o'clock the tenantry, by Lord Sheffield's invitation, sat down to a sumptuous dinner at the Sheffield Arms. The room was decorated for the occasion with banners, laurels and other characteristic embellishments. At the back of the chair was a large flag, with the arms and quarterings of the family, which was the more interesting from being the needlework and design of the Countess of Sheffield. Over the mantelpiece was the initial 'P' at the foot of which was inscribed 'Loyal to his Queen, true to his country,' the whole worked in laurel leaves upon a pink ground. Opposite the chair were the arms and supporters of the Sheffield family, and in each recess were the military banners of the late Earl of Sheffield. On the arrival of the company, they were conducted to the reception room, where they all most cordially expressed their congratulations to Lord Pevensey on this auspicious occasion.

Among the guests was W.E Baxter, the Lewes printer and publisher whose books on Lewes and Sussex by the Rev. T. W. Horsfield are much sought after today.

Viscount Pevensey made an 'eloquent address' to the guests concluding with his wish 'to cement those amicable relations which ought to exist between landlord and tenant and which I fancy do exist, or we would not be associated together this evening'.

James and John Comber held the tenancy until 1871 when another Comber, Susannah, became the licensee and one of the rooms behind the newly-built pavilions in Sheffield Park was specially for her use. She was praised for the 'excellence of her catering' for one of Lord Sheffield's XI matches against Alfred Shaw's XI.

Viscount Pevensey, the future third Lord Sheffield, celebrates his 21st birthday on January 18th, 1853 at the Sheffield Arms. The large 'P' for Pevensey was made with laurel leaves. *Illustrated London News*

AUSTRALIAN CRICKETERS AT SHEFFIELD PARK

Richard Welfare took over the tenancy in 1886 and stayed 23 years. His catering skills also seem to have been much in demand for the Sheffield Park cricket matches.

The third Lord Sheffield was passionate about the game. He developed an existing pitch that had been created for him when he was 13 years old and on holiday from Eton, by his father, the second Earl of Sheffield. Later it became a world-class ground. The Australians would frequently open their tour here and came five times between 1884 and 1896 to play against Lord Sheffield's XI. This often included the legendary WG Grace, A Shaw, CB Fry and KS Ranjitsinhji.

A view from Lord Sheffield's pavilion of the match between Lord Sheffield's XI and the Australian in 1884. *Photo by kind permission of Peter Wigan*

Richard Welfare was also called upon to cater for many events other than cricket - Lord Sheffield had wide interests. He once invited 1000 children from London with 100 adults and Welfare provided the tea. Another time there was a mile-long picnic table for Sunday School children. In 1889 Welfare served lunch in the Sheffield Park pavilion for the crew of the Heloise, Lord Sheffield's yacht. A year later, the Sussex Volunteer Force, formed to fight the French in case of an invasion, came to Sheffield Park for one of their Field Days. Volunteers from all over the country came too, and Welfare supplied the non-commissioned officers and men with bread, cheese and ale, it was said, in less than 20 minutes.

His catering must have been good because in 1894 when Lord Sheffield invited a Nottingham Forest football club and the Sussex Martlets to compete at Sheffield Park, the teams were entertained by Lord Sheffield after the match at the Sheffield Arms. Host Welfare was said to have provided an excellent repast.

It was on May 11th, 1896 that the Prince of Wales, later Edward VII, attended the opening match of the ninth Australian tour and 30,000 people came to watch. To Lord Sheffield's disappointment the Prince of Wales said he was not able to stay the night and had to return to London, but some of the Australian team stayed at the Sheffield Arms. Lord Sheffield had enlarged the building for them.

Landlords Harry and Margery Grace 1944. *Photo by kind permission of Roy Lingham.*

Richard Welfare left in 1909, the same year Lord Sheffield died at the age of 77. In 1920 the pub was sold to Tamplin's Brewery.

There were five more licensees before Frederick Edwards arrived in 1929. He and his wife stayed for six years and the pub had a new name: the Sheffield Arms Hotel. The Public and Saloon bars were on the left, the lounge and smaller bar on the right. There were eight bedrooms with six semi-invalids living there whom Mrs Edwards looked after. She also provided teas at the Sheffield Park cricket ground on Sundays when the gardens were open to the public.

There were darts teams at the pub but no transport for the members until they found a small firm in Ardingly, a nearby village, that had two or three army coaches. The Monday night team played in the Mid Sussex League; the Friday night team played in the Forest Row and the

District League. There were matches, too, for the Coronation Cup given by Mrs Soames of Sheffield Park.

After Mrs Edwards left in 1935, there were again changes of tenants: William Gander (1935), Thomas Bayes (1935 to 1937), Arthur Huggons (1937 to 1939), Ernest Swaby (1939 to 1940). In 1940 Mr and Mrs Grace arrived.

The Sheffield Arms darts team 1951, Roy Lingham, front row, right. *Photo by kind permission of Roy Lingham*

SECOND WORLD WAR

At the beginning of the Second World War Sheffield Park was requisitioned by the War Office and Nissen huts were erected in the woods and around the grounds for thousands of troops stationed there. The Welsh Regiment came first and a Sergeant and two Privates used to walk down to the Sheffield Arms every day for a pint with their Welsh mascot, The Goat, dressed in regimental colours. Then came the Pandas, an English regiment, (the divisional sign of the 9th armoured division). After them there were three Canadian regiments: Le Regiment de la Chaudière, French speakers from Quebec; the 3rd Canadian Tank Regiment, the first to land in Normandy on D-Day June 6, 1944; and the Cape Breton Highlanders, a Canadian infantry regiment that was in England for two years before fighting in Italy and northern Holland. Some took part in the 1942 ill-fated raid on Dieppe.

Many used to drink at the Sheffield Arms and Roy Lingham, whose farm was next door, remembers how the Canadians were quick to draw their knives. 'In the finish they had to be parted,' he said. 'The Cape Breton Highlanders were allowed to drink at The Arms but the French Canadians had to go to The Griffin or the Rose and Crown in Fletching. They were all so eager to get to war, they used to fight among themselves, often outside the Sheffield Arms. I think they found the beer too strong!'

The regulars used the Public Bar, sitting on their own benches, drinking and smoking their pipes. The troops drank in the lounge and saloon bars and local young men were allowed to sit with them.

When a V1 flying bomb exploded in Sheffield Green, it killed two cart horses but six bullocks lying near them survived.

Roy Lingham joined the Home Guard (immortalised in the TV series 'Dad's Army'). Writing many years later in the Fletching Parish magazine, he remembers how the local group started:

It was in May 1940 that the call came for volunteers to join in the defence of our country, so most of the men and youths of the Parish stepped forward. We started off as the Local Defence Volunteer D Division and for two or three nights a week we had to watch out for enemy action around the parish and report anything we saw to the police. After a few weeks, things got a little bit better organised and we became the Home Guard attached to the 17th Battalion Royal Sussex D Company. There were seven of us but I am the only one left. Sometimes the regular army took us to Ashdown Forest for rifle practice, and we also had a small range of our own in the old brick-yard down Ketches Road, half a mile away from Sheffield Green. We practised with a revolver, sten gun and 22 calibre rifles.

There was also a Searchlight Unit. That was stationed in a field near the Sheffield Arms, and the men used the pub a good deal. They had had a field telephone installed there and, if a warning or 'Take Post' came through, they could get back to the searchlight very quickly.

There were lectures from the regular army in the nearby Reading Room, a tin hut that became known as the Home Guard Head-quarters, and there were always five Privates and an NCO on duty until daylight. There would also be two men checking peoples' identities on Sheffield Green or at the Reading Room. On Sunday morning there was drill in the Park or railway station. The men used to drink in the Sheffield Arms and, with food rationing, quite a few boys used to catch rabbits, and give a couple of brace to The Arms for a few pints.

In 1942 the Home Guard held their Christmas dinner there. Fruit for the pudding came from the Canadian army cooks, rabbit stew from poachers who traded rabbits for beer. The dinner was given by the tenants Mr and Mrs Grace. One of the soldiers, a Cape Breton

Highlander named Red Gordon MacQuarrie, was a good violinist and piper and used to play his fiddle in the pub in return for drinks.

The Home Guard Christmas dinner at the Sheffield Arms 1942

Photograph by kind permission of Edward Reeves Photography

NEW DEVELOPMENTS

Landlords Harry and Margery Grace stayed until 1947. Only two more tenants were to follow until the 99-year lease held by Tamplin's Brewery ran out. They were Edgar Boyd (1947 to 1956) and Percy Clayton (1956 to 1965). In 1969 The Sheffield Arms was put up for sale again.

Tamplin's representative applied to Uckfield Licensing Justices for a protection order for the licence to be transferred to him as caretaker of the property until it was sold, and this was agreed. The chairman hoped 'it would not be sold as it was such a fine old property with a typically English setting'.

It was empty for 18 months until it was bought in 1970 by the Halland Group of companies, who spent £68,000 renovating it. On February 17 there was a pre-opening night party with business colleagues, the architect, designers, local residents and the Press invited for a buffet supper. There were two new restaurants: The Sheffield Grill and the Regency Room. The Sheffield Grill was in Jacobean style, with tapestries, high-backed settles and pewter pots. It specialised in steaks, and customers could see the food being prepared at the end of the restaurant. A three-course meal cost 30 shillings. The Regency Room had an island bar and period fireplace – the menus were à la carte with higher prices and more choice.

Later in the year they opened a Midnight Room for two hundred dancers, dining and cabaret. Everything did not go right on the first night and guests were plunged into darkness by a faulty fuse. 'Luckily we don't cook by electricity,' the manager, Mr Fred Croker, explained to the guests, many of whom thought it was an opening-night gimmick.

The restaurant with its twice-weekly dinner-dances was very popular and guests included TV comedian Ronnie Corbett, Mary Bryant of

Coronation Street, opera singer Owen Brannigan, and Ray Barrett of TVS The Trouble Shooters. There were plans for a motel to be opened and package tours for wedding receptions.

But things did not go well for Halland Hotels and a year later the Sheffield Arms was taken over by Selected Hotels.

'We come from the village of St. James in London to the heart of Sussex with the sincere hope that we will make a tremendous success here,' Mr Simon Broome, managing director of London's Stafford Hotel (part of Selected Hotels), told food and wine writers, wine merchants and caterers invited to meet the new management.

Their future plans included a series of gastronomic weekends with classical dishes and wine from wine-growing regions of Europe, art exhibitions, fashion shows and antique fairs.

Tenants Mr & Mrs Croker 1970.
Photo: Sussex Express

There were à la carte menus and a set-price £2.30 Saturday night dinner dance. Sunday lunch cost £1.25. There were plans for wedding receptions, banquets, conferences, discos.

But, 25 years later in 1996, the Sheffield Arms, with its historic name and after over two hundred years as a coaching inn, working pub, hotel, disco, jazz club and restaurant, was forced to close its doors for good. It lay empty for eighteen months until it was bought by Michael Clifford and Tracy Thomson who gave it its new name (Trading Boundaries) and breathed new life into the old building.

They opened for business in 1998 with a retail section of vintage Indian furniture, fine art, home furnishing, live music, courtyard shopping and a café/bar, two hundred and twenty years after the first Lord Sheffield thought it would be a good idea and make economic sense to open an inn here.

Selected Hotels opening night 1970. Simon Broome, far right. *Photo: Sussex Express*

GHOSTS

The building's ghosts described by those who have seen them.

Kristan Fawcus, former General Manager

Thomas Horton and his wife lived here in the 1800s. I believe Thomas was a groundskeeper and the rumour has it that his wife killed herself when quite young. She hanged herself from a tree in the back garden and he found her. They said it was something to do with the fact that she couldn't have children. He went on living there but was very bitter about the situation. He allegedly haunts the back bedroom on the second floor with Murphy, a black cat with a very curly tail.

Murphy is still seen and heard by many people. I've heard it myself and seen a dog chase after it, even though it's not there. You can hear it on the landing sometimes.

There used to be a dog here called Ringo that belonged to Tracy Thomson and he was here for fifteen years. He often used to go after the cat, or bark, always in the same place and I've seen it out of the corner of my eye. Then the realisation kicks in and I ask myself: why is there a cat on the stairs – no one has a cat here?

One day I was standing in the restaurant and Ringo was racing around, and I heard a voice whisper in my ear 'crazy dog'. There are a few other things that have occurred in the restaurant. There is a thin white figure that appears throwing things, normally between the pillars. It's like somebody is taking a pot shot at you. When you see it, it disappears. Quite a few people have seen that. Sometimes it whispers the names of staff into their ears. I guess it's because the names are said so often when they talk to each other. The person who'd heard the whisper would then ask if anyone had said anything to them. It's intriguing really because the restaurant wasn't built until the 70s.

In one of the back rooms there's sometimes a kind of swishing-past sound, as if someone is trying to grasp you or get your attention by flicking you. You feel a whoosh of air. It used to feel quite sinister but now it seems to have gone.

There's definitely a ghost of a child downstairs who is known to arrange little things on the top of furniture. I've felt him tickle my hand and touch my back pocket, like a child tapping his mum or dad trying to get their attention. There was once a dumb-waiter which went from the ground floor to the very top, but that was cut off and turned into a staircase. Allegedly a child fell down the stairs and died and then they blocked the stairs off. There's now a cupboard there. Everyone used to refer to this cupboard where the cleaning products are kept as the ghost cupboard. And I started to get feelings of a very innocent, very tickly, mischievous child. There is still a spirit or apparition there in that time period – for a ghost, the building is still the same regardless of whether anything has been changed.

When there were maids here, they lived upstairs on the top floor and there was a staircase to it. The maids used to come down that way but when the stairs were blocked off they couldn't do so. Their ghosts do get down sometimes but seem to prefer to stay upstairs. They don't seem to like noise and when we have music here, they move things around. They used to stack up the furniture, but this doesn't happen any more.

Tracy Thomson, joint owner, Trading Boundaries

The building does have a character of its own and I've seen the most extraordinary things. A customer once came up to me and said: "it might sound strange because I don't know you, but I get a strong feeling your grandmother is trying to contact you." My grandmother had died that year. From doing some research with a medium I was told that there were other people living in the building and they weren't very happy, that there wasn't enough space for them, that the place where they were was full of brightly coloured things. In fact, there was a cupboard which was full of brightly coloured papier-mâché plates.

After that we always called that the ghost cupboard. We also had a lot of activity on the top floor and I felt quite uncomfortable going there.

There was a routine at the end of the day for turning off the lights. All the switches are in different places and one night I could see through to the next room which is near the ghost cupboard. I saw and heard a light switch I hadn't got to, being flicked off and a foot-step on the carpet. I thought there must be someone still there. There was a chap living there at the time and I called up to him but he didn't reply. He was actually in the shower. He went and got a baseball bat in case there was an intruder, but there wasn't anyone there.

On another occasion when I was living in the building, I was watching TV in my lounge, chatting to a friend on the phone with my back to the ghost cupboard. At that time there was a big piece of mirror glass leaning against a wall and out from behind me, came an elderly lady in what you can only describe as a maid's uniform. It was a black dress with a white apron. She came out from where the ghost cupboard is and walked across the room. I saw her in the mirror. She went over to the far wall, picked something up and left, like it was the most natural thing in the world. Not a sound. It was extraordinary.

Some nights when I was trying to go to sleep, it was like being on a busy road. I heard car doors in the car park outside, footsteps on the gravel but there was no one there. And there were constant things going past me in the room. One night I sat up and shouted: 'go away and leave me alone, I need to sleep.' And at that point I swear a cat jumped on to my bed (I didn't have a cat). I said: 'you can clear off as well.' And it did.

Ghost hunters come here to practise smudging, lighting a bunch of dried herbs which then smoulder. We have groups of ladies – I find them in the back field – standing in a circle on the points of a pentacle. They told me they felt they had been drawn here to release spirits. They clocked up some activity but, to be honest, I think it was a bit vague.

MEMORIES

Local people remember the Sheffield Arms and life in Sheffield Green.

Roy Lingham was born in 1922 and lived at Vigoes Farm next to the Sheffield Arms from 1934 until he moved to Newick in 2000.

Sheffield Green on the A275 is the piece of land in front of the Sheffield Arms and at one time it had seven oaks and two chestnut trees. This land on each side of the road up to Furners Green we called the Common but it was really Manorial Waste looked after by the current Lord of the Manor. There were two mounting blocks there and the part where the Sheffield Arms sign was swinging weighed over three hundredweight.

For nearly eighty years I lived in the farm next door to it which at that time went with the Sheffield Arms. That was the place where they changed horses for the coach which went from Croydon, via East Grinstead, Lewes and Brighton.

From 1922 they held an annual Little Fair here, with swings and a hand-turned roundabout. In Pound Farm's field opposite, there were sack, and wheelbarrow and egg and spoon races. I remember one year my Mum winning a three-legged race with Mr. Percy Mepham of Ketches Farm up the road.

When Frederick Edwards and his wife came to be licensees in 1929, the bar was redecorated but it never lasted long because so many customers used to smoke the old tobacco in their pipes and it discoloured the ceiling. Mrs Edwards used to do the cream teas in the Pavilion when Sheffield Park was open to the public. Their son, Frank, lost his life in Dunkirk.

We used to take milk from the farm to The Arms night and morning. We'd strain it, put it in a cooler, then a billycan, however much they wanted, usually about half a gallon every day when Mrs. Edwards was looking after the semi-invalids; her husband didn't have anything to do with that side of things. The Dig for Victory campaign began in the Second World War and the grass tennis courts and the bowling green at the back of The Arms (where the restaurant is today) were dug up to grow vegetables.

At that time the present courtyard was our cattle yard. Two girls from the Land Army, Kay and Eileen, came to help in the Market Garden and I think one stayed at the Sheffield Arms. They were both fashion models and they said one spent most of the time behind the bar!

1930s grass tennis court and bowling green that were dug up to grow potatoes in World War Two.

When I was in the Home Guard, I used to go to The Arms for an evening drink. The public bar had all the farmers and temporary workers and several well-known people went there: Hannen Swaffer, the cartoonist, and Dirk Bogarde's Mum and Dad used to sit in the saloon. Dirk wasn't really interested in the girls but Maggie, his mother, she was a lad. Her husband was Arts Editor of The Times.

Members of The Guinea Pig club came too. This was established in 1941 at the Queen Victoria Hospital in East Grinstead, for airmen whose faces and hands had been severely burned. Some had no faces at all. The famous surgeon, Archibald McIndoe, had developed treatments for reconstructing them at the hospital.

Some people in East Grinstead shunned them because they were so disfigured, but Mr. Grace decided he would give them a social evening every month at the Sheffield Arms and sent his wife to the hospital to fetch them. When she couldn't go, he asked me and two others with cars to drive them. The airmen were so friendly with lots of jokes and they mixed with all the locals. Mrs Grace laid on sandwiches as best she could with the rationing on.

Land girls at the Sheffield Arms 1942.
Photo by kind permission of Peter Richardson

One of the boys, he used to like to sit by me in the passenger seat of the car, and his name was also Roy. He was an Air Gunner in an RAF Handley Page 'Hampden', (a British twin- engine medium bomber) and was shot down in 1941 somewhere in Kent. When he was due to be discharged from the hospital, Mr Grace trained him to be a barman at the Sheffield Arms and he was there for about 12 months.

After the war there was clay pigeon shooting at The Arms. Once a month the Sheffield Park Keepers used to have a little kitty, half a crown or a florin. It was just for themselves and one or two local farmers. But when it got bigger, the pellets were dropping down on to the Fletching road. One day Bert Meads, the policeman, said to Stan Setford who lived next to us, that they'd have to stop. "Someone might have pellets falling on their heads and think they were being shot at," he said. "They'd have to do something about it." Stan offered to hold the shoots at Northall Farm, which he owned further up the Fletching road, and that's what happened.

Bert always used to come to the Sheffield Arms kitchen for his regular pint and it was also the meeting place for the Danehill and Fletching policemen. They'd come round the back at six o'clock in the morning where my mother always had a cup of tea or coffee for them. That's how the local news got about. Everyone knew them. They didn't leave their bikes outside; they'd go in the back way – they didn't want anyone to know they were there.

Before mains water was piped into the area, the Sheffield Arms got water from its own well in the cellar. You went into the kitchen, up a little passageway and then down some steps. It wasn't the main beer cellar; they just kept odds and ends there. At one time The Arms had water laid on from the Sheffield Park estate. It was all gravity fed, no pressure, beautiful spring water. The Canadians were the first to lay mains water from North Chailey; it now comes from Wych Cross. There were six wells in the area at that time.

Electricity came to The Arms in 1956. I remember it well. When my family came to live in Vigoes farm in 1934, they had their own generator with batteries that had to be charged up. There was a little old lady in Newick, a Miss Trickie, who used to run a van and she'd bring her accumulator to The Arms and charge sixpence a week for recharging. With the arrival of mains electricity, we could plug the radio in.

(Before radios were electric, the source of power was an accumulator, something like a car battery and these had to be recharged from time to time. Peter Richardson, Pest Control Officer at the Sheffield Park Estate, remembers Miss Trickie. He explains: the dud accumulators went in one side of the van and the re-charged ones in the other, but there was no proper separation between them. Sometimes Miss Trickie would leave you with a dud one and when my Dad went to turn the radio on, it was clear something was wrong. I then had to cycle over to Newick to get a replacement.)

Bert Setford, our neighbour, always said there was a curse on the Sheffield Arms and anyone who ran it just for food wouldn't succeed. Before it was bought by Michael Clifford and Tracy Thomson, the pub had so many licensees, perhaps there was something in that old curse!

The Old Surrey & Burstow Hunt at the Sheffield Arms
Photo by kind permission of Roy Lingham

I've seen so many changes there. There was a Mr Simpson who came from Kent. He had the idea of turning it into a disco. One night they had a coach load from Brighton and one from London and they clashed and all hell broke loose. They set one of the coaches alight and Derek (my son) and myself stood there with a shotgun. We wanted to stop them coming into the farm because of the cows and all the haystacks we had. Actually, we didn't have anything in the guns – it was just a deterrent!

At one time the Old Surrey and Burstow hunt met here. It was wonderful. The huntsmen in their red coats, the followers and the dogs wandering around. Then you'd see someone come out with a tray going round and handing out the drinks.

Bert Setford, 90-year-old wood-cutter in 1978
Photo: Tony Tree

Bert Setford, a woodcutter, was 90 years old in 1978 when Angela Wigglesworth interviewed him about his memories of the day in 1896 when the Prince of Wales (later Edward VII) came to Sheffield Park.

Did I go to see the match? Well, more or less, you see, but we were more interested in the Prince of Wales. He came into Sheffield Park station. It was a sight, you know. He came in May and the children from round here brought all the wild flowers they could find a day or so before. They took them into the stable and the flowers were all bunched up and roped together and the children lined the street from the station to Sheffield Park. The ropes were to keep the people back. My father worked in the brickyard and was chosen for the special police. He walked out among the crowd to follow the Prince and, oh lord, it was a sight you know. Father told us where to go to get a good view and we could see him coming all the way. He got a grey trilby hat on with this large white carnation in his buttonhole. He came in a carriage and pair – there were no motors then.

When the Prince of Wales got to the cricket ground, he stopped and told his Lordship (Sheffield) he was so surprised. He never thought he would get such a welcome coming to such a little old country place like this at that time of day and all the flowers. He was highly delighted. "But now I've got to disappoint you," he said, because he couldn't stop the night because he got some official business in London. That was how that was. He had rook pie, that was a delicacy at that time of day. At night-time we had all those magic lights.

It was a great disappointment for Lord Sheffield that the Prince of Wales didn't stay the night. They said it cost him thousands and thousands of pounds for him to come down.

Some of the cricketers slept at the Mansion but most of them slept at the Sheffield Arms and the Griffin. They were met at the station and taken there by the carriages. Lord Sheffield used to keep some fine horses and had coachmen.

Barbara Johnson, formerly Barbara Brewin, 81 years old, now lives in Uckfield.

My mother and I lived with my grandparents at the Sheffield Park Hotel, as it was known then, from 1937 to 1940 when my grand-father – Ernest Millard Swaby – was the licensee. He was married to Lucille Swaby, known as Lucy, and their son Malcolm lived there from 1935 to 1940. He was sadly killed in Dunkirk.

My grandfather attended to the clearing work and maintenance of the garden and hotel, while my grandmother looked after kitchen duties. I remember there was a butcher's block and she used to cut up meat with a big chopper. She always had a glass of Guinness or stout beside her. Often there were rabbits hanging up for her to skin or cook. My mother helped with the cleaning and worked in the bar.

My grandmother had a piano in the corner of the large room on the right at the top of the main staircase leading from the front hall. There was a wooden staircase from the bar area to the top floor that was, or had been, the live-in staff accommodation. I remember a toilet with a large scrubbed wall-to-wall seat.

My grandfather was always puzzled by a window which is blanked out and can be seen from the outside but not from the inside. From the outside it is white and can still be seen today on the front of the building.

Before the Second World War there were many visitors to the hotel who came for holidays and weekends. I loved looking at the big black cars that arrived at the hotel with beautifully dressed ladies and gentlemen.

When my grandparents left the hotel in 1940, my mother and I were offered half of Vigoes farmhouse next door owned by Don Lingham, and we lived there a further two years. I used to go into the large barn at the back where big bins of corn were stored, and chase the mice around. My father, George Brewin, worked in London and would only visit us occasionally.

Kristan Fawcus - former general manager

I remember a visitor coming in one day – her mother had found a set of three old books that were like the AA Guides today, including information about where to bring your horses and carriage on your travels. Book Two covered the south-east and the visitor wanted to see if the places mentioned still existed. The Sheffield Arms had been highly rated because of how well the horses were looked after in the stable next door. A lot of taverns would take customers' money and just give the horses old straw or dirty water. At the Sheffield Arms, the Guide stated, they actually cared about the animals, brushed them for you and got a five-star rating.

We have two cellars here, one for beer, one for odds and ends and it's said there was once a smugglers' tunnel here. It was supposed to go from this cellar and under the fields over to Colin Godmans, to smuggle French brandy brought up the River Ouse from the coast. Trying to find out if a tunnel actually did exist, it's said they once put a goose down there with a hound to chase it, but I don't think that proved anything. But there are markings on a stone wall which look like something may have once been there.

Julian Foreman was about 20 years old when he worked as a barman at the Sheffield Arms Night Club in the 1980s. He now lives in Uckfield.

The Night Club at that time was called Hillies and Chris Hill was the DJ with Pete Tonk who later worked at Radio One. They played Blues, Soul, Latin Jazz and Funk. I remember Freddie and the Doughnuts who played in the style of Madness. They came on stage wearing trilby hats and the lead singer carried a briefcase. It was full of doughnuts which he threw at everyone. There were doughnuts everywhere. When the Sheffield Arms changed hands, the bar was renamed The Philadelphia Connection – one of the owners had a share in a pub in Philadelphia, and he opened up a burger bar with American food. There was a Night Club on Fridays, Saturdays and Sundays and lots of people came. After the fight (referred to by Roy Lingham) between the coach load of police cadets and a coach from Brighton, the locals wanted the place closed down; it was too noisy. It finished the Sheffield Arms.

Philip Gregory lived with his parents and three brothers in Yew Tree Cottage near the Sheffield Arms.

I was fourteen in 1983 when I first went down to the Sheffield Arms and asked for work. I wanted to earn some pocket money and they gave me a job helping to look after the three donkeys they kept in the stables. One of them, called The Clot, was owned by the comedian Jimmy Edwards whose brother farmed in Fletching. I used to clean out their mess and on Saturday mornings I cleared up the car park too – I'd sometimes find money that Night Club customers had dropped getting into their taxis!

In the late 80s we had a pool team at the Sheffield Arms and it was in the Lewes League. We played many of the local pubs.

Jimmy Edwards, the comedian, with his donkey at the Sheffield Arms, and landlord, Bill Sargent (right) 1951. The little boy on the donkey was Derek Lingham. *Photo by kind permission of Roy Lingham*

John Howe lived at Walkwood Cottage on the Fletching road from 1974 to 1986. His father, Bill Howe, was Resident Agent of the Sheffield Park Estate when it was owned by Captain Arthur Soames, until it was sold in 1953. John farmed at Home Farm, Sheffield Park until 2005. He now lives in Lincolnshire with his wife, Nicky.

During the 60s we used to buy ice creams from the kitchen door of the Sheffield Arms. In the early 70s they did dinner dances in the new function room at the rear. Both my sisters' after-wedding parties were held there in 1971 and 1972 – I seem to remember the food and service were pretty dreadful on both occasions! In the early 80s the function room, which by then had half an American car protruding from a wall (The Philadelphia Connection), had a Saturday night disco attracting bus loads from Croydon and Crawley. We were living at Winters Cottage then and we would lie in bed and hear rivals threatening each other with knives; we understood there were the occasional stabbings. My first job on Sunday morning was to shovel up all the mess in our driveway before our children went out to play.

During the 70s and 80s the National Farmers' Union used to hold its branch meetings in the room to the right of the front door. In the room on the left were photos of the Sheffield Park estate on the walls. In particular there were a number of photos of Lord Sheffield's cricket matches. I believe these are now displayed in the new pavilion on the old cricket ground in the Park which is used by the Armadillo Cricket Club. I was an early member and I once played there.

When nowadays my family meet up in the area, usually for funerals, we always go to The Arms (now called Trading Boundaries) for a coffee first. A good coffee and a cooked breakfast go down well after our journey from Lincolnshire. I am envious of the concerts they now have as they are often 'my music'. I did try for tickets for Steve Hackett last autumn, but all the seats and meals were gone and I wasn't going to drive for four hours and stand all evening!

Enid Wood, born in nearby Sliders Lane, now lives at Furners Green.

There used to be a dominoes team at The Arms and they'd play in the Public Bar every night of the week: Eddie Wood (my father-in-law), was a brickie employed by the Sheffield Park Estate; Bill Daniel, he worked at the saw mills; Frank Gilham (not sure where he worked); Bill Burley was the second underkeeper on the Estate. There was a darts team, too, and the winner got a gallon of beer.

After the war thousands of German prisoners of war were based in the camp at Sheffield Park.

Maurice Forbes-Wood

I lived at Chequers, one of three cottages just up the road from The Arms. I remember the Little Fair on Sheffield Green: the girls all used to dress up and there was always a tug-of-war team. My mother, Ruby Wood, and my aunt Kit were chefs at The Arms and they cooked good English food – countryman cooking, they called it. My brother, John, who died, worked there, too, and I remember Mr Grace, the tenant, calling out to him one day: "I want chicken for tonight. Kill that one over there." And he did.

Andrew Hudson contributes news items to the Fletching Parish magazine that appeared in the Sussex Express a century ago.

DANCE AT FLETCHING, (Sussex Express 14 November 1919).

An enjoyable dance took place at the Sheffield Arms Hotel, to wind up the season of the Sheffield Green Tennis Club, the court being on the Sheffield Arms Hotel lawn. The members and friends owe the success of the dance to Mr. and Mrs. Monk, who threw open their large dining room for the occasion and also undertook the management of the refreshments. There were between 70 and 80 present and dancing was kept up until 1 o'clock. Honorary tickets were taken by Mr. and Mrs. A.G. Soames of Sheffield Park, Dr. and Mrs. Gravely, Miss Attenborough, Mr. and Mrs. H. Hall, Mr. and Mrs. Parks, Mr. F. Martin, Mr. and Mrs. Pickwell and Mrs. Eggleton. Over 30 dances were indulged in. Mr. H. Stevenson, of Fletching, carrying on the duties of M.C. in a very creditable manner. The members are indebted to Miss Skinner, Station House, who took a very active part in helping to arrange the dance and also for acting as Hon. Secretary to the Club during the past season. Excellent music was supplied by Mrs. Brown (piano), and Mr. Wood of Newick (violin).

FLETCHING AND DISTRICT (Sussex Express 7th October 1900)

CORN, ROOT. BUTTER, HOP, POULTRY SHOW AND PLOUGHING MATCH.

THE 33rd ANNUAL EXHIBITION WILL BE HELD ON THE GREEN

in front of the "Sheffield Arms. Fletching on FRIDAY OCTOBER 14th

Mr. W. Goring, of the Uckfield Agricultural College, will send an Exhibit of Fruit, and several

kinds of SUGAR BEET, grown at the College

8.30 am to 12.30 Ploughing Match.

12.30 pm Open judging of Teams

1 pm Open judging of Horses.

1 to 3pm Show Open to Visitors.

2 pm Auction Sale of the whole of the Exhibits (except Horses and Poultry).

ANNUAL DINNER AT THE SHEFFIELD ARMS

Chair will be taken by the PRESIDENT (A. G. SOAMES Esq., J.P., D.L.), at 4 0'clock.

GEO. FENNER.

WHAT NEXT?

In the 1990s a building firm approached Tracy Thomson who had a property development company in Brighton, to ask for advice about dealing with a listed building. She explains what happened:

Our company, Clifford Properties, was very well-known for our conservation work. They told us they had come across a lovely site that they wanted to buy for plots for new-build homes but didn't know how to deal with the listed building. Would I advise them on renovating it and separate it into apartments? I did.

But their purchase didn't go anywhere because they discovered they wouldn't be given planning permission.

At that time Michael Clifford had started Trading Boundaries, selling Indian furniture from a small barn in Dormansland, a village near where they lived in Sharpthorne. He had named it Trading Boundaries after his previous freight company: Aerial Boundaries.

His mother was born in India, his grandfather had been a missionary there and he had visited it in his teens. In the 1990s, he became aware of exclusive shops in the Notting Hill area of London selling Indian furniture at very high prices and thought there must be something in this furniture business. In 1996 he took a break from the property development company which he and Tracy ran together, and got on a plane to India. He spent three and a half weeks looking for furniture he could sell in the UK and eventually found what he wanted.

'I knew about getting things from A to B because of my freight business,' he said, 'and with the arrival of my first Indian container we set up shop in the barn, opening two hours a week at week-ends. We advertised it locally: "Come to importers direct and save pounds," and people did. After a few months I advertised it nationally and our income went up threefold. They took over another barn three times as big'.

But the barns did not have retail planning permission, they could only be used for light industrial work. They now not only needed more space to trade from, Tracy said, but one that was more conducive for bringing clients to and where they could be open full-time. They found the Sheffield Arms had come back on the market.

'It was kind of serendipitous,' she said. 'I had a very detailed knowledge of the building because of the survey I'd done the year before for the new-build company'.

It had been empty for eighteen months – no one had known what to do with it. It was too big for a pub with the drink driving laws and very run down. But it would be an ideal showroom, they thought, for their Indian furniture.

They bought the Sheffield Arms in April 1998, opened for business in October that year, and gave the building a new name: Trading Boundaries.

'We managed to get an investor to help us,' Michael said, 'and I stood on a soap box at a parish council meeting, arguing for retail permission. "We know you don't know who we are," I told them. "But this place needs a future and we don't think a pub is the future. We would like to try retail."

There was a loophole in the law at that time - if pubs did not work, they could be converted to retail. They got planning permission to convert the pub into a retail business.

The building was not in a good state. 'The previous owners hadn't been able to look after it,' Tracy said. 'There weren't any gutters for a start. We had cast-iron ones made. Everything had to be right for a Listed building. I could quite understand why companies would not have been able to do this because of the financial commitment.

'I was a bit anxious about it,' she admitted. 'Michael wasn't. It was a large project for us at the time. Our furniture business was in its infancy though it was going great. It was quite a commitment. It would have been a struggle to keep the Sheffield Arms going as a pub. It's a big building and not attached to a village. Everyone has to drive to get here.

'When we first opened the showrooms, we just had a little kettle in a cupboard to make tea and coffee. It wasn't until 2005 that we came up with the idea of having a café – we did tea, coffee and cake. It was tiny, just eight tables. The rest of the area was the showroom. My brother was in charge of that and my mother started the café. It went from strength to strength and took over more space from the shop. Three years later we extended the kitchen and started doing lunches'.

When they bought the property, Roy Lingham's dairy farm was next door but in 2002 he decided to retire. Tracy and Michael bought the barns and built a courtyard there with six boutique-style shops around it, selling flowers, clothes, handicrafts, toys and wine.

'But over the years, with the advent of the internet, people's spending habits changed, and it became harder to make a success of the shops,' Michael admitted. 'With that side of the business going down, Tracy and I had to think hard about what to do and we decided on accommodation. We would convert the little shops into a Boutique Coaching Inn and do weddings on a more regular basis'.

Planning permission came through in May 2020 and permission to make internal alterations five months later.

'I am really excited about our plans', Tracy said. 'They have been on the back burner, or maybe on the horizon, for some time. To have found an alternative use for our award-winning courtyard development has been wonderful. After all, it began as a coaching inn all those years ago' (They were runner-up in the Sussex Conservation Heritage Awards in 2006).

About 18 years ago, they started barbecue weekends with live music. It was the beginning of their popular music evenings with world-famous musicians coming to play: Steve Hackett, Rick Wakeman, Steve Howe, Greg Lake and Carl Palmer among them. Bands included Focus, Renaissance, Caravan, Brand New Heavies, The Blockheads.

The concerts have now dovetailed into their need to provide accommodation. 'Customers come a long way to hear them,' said Michael. 'One lady comes all the way from Japan, others from America. With our boutique rooms we will have somewhere for them to stay.

'It is the perfect place for music – the quality of the acoustics is stunning. We won an award in the Classic Rock magazine for having the finest venue in the UK after the Albert Hall. The customers voted – the Albert Hall just have more of them!

'If you go to the theatre for opera and live music, generally speaking you sit in a row. Here you can watch something with a glass of wine or beer and connect with your friends while you're eating. It's the same with opera. The singers use the whole restaurant as their canvass – they can be singing and acting all around you – that makes it very special'.

Trading Boundaries also represents the artist Roger Dean, well-known for his posters and album covers. 'He lives nearby and used to come in for hot chocolate.' Michael said. 'We became friends and suggested we sell some of his artwork. It goes very much hand-in-hand with the music we're doing'.

The future?

They will continue with the café during the day and keep the retail side with the Indian furniture, but the weddings and accommodation will be the driving force.

'We are very mindful of future generations and that we are just a point in history', Michael said. 'Having to close down for Covid-19 has given us a life-time opportunity to look at the building in depth. We have discovered the original Georgian shutters, all oiled and sealed by layers of paint. We understand the fabric of the building now and how things were before Victorian vandalism: they chopped off the whole of an inglenook fireplace and there was a bread oven next to it. We had to wall it up again – we needed the retail space – but future generations can explore it. I feel very proud of the fact that we have been here longer than anyone else'.

'Working in such an historic place, it's hard sometimes not to take it for granted,' Tracy said. 'But the building does have a character of its own and sometimes you have a day when you look at it and think how very, very lucky we are to be here'.

**Michael Clifford & Tracy Thomson,
the present owners of Trading Boundaries**

SHEFFIELD ARMS THROUGH THE CENTURIES

Sheffield Arms with Great Oak, mid 19th century *Photo by kind permission of Peter Richardson*

42

Sheffield Arms with horse & cart, c1890s *Photo by kind permission of Peter Richardson*

Sheffield Arms with coach and horses, c1900.
Photo from the late Derek Rawlings of the Danehill Parish Historical Society

Sheffield Arms c 1910 *Photo by kind permission of Roger Packham*

Sheffield Arms, view from the bowling green, 1920s

46

Sheffield Arms Hotel, c1940. *Photo by kind permission of Roy Lingham*

Sheffield Arms c 1944, *Photo by kind permission of Roy Lingham*

48

Sheffield Arms in the 1960s. *Photo by kind permission of Roy Lingham*

ACKNOWLEDGEMENTS

I would like to thank the following people who generously gave me their knowledge of the Sheffield Arms:

Christopher Whittick, whose detailed research of the Sheffield Arms published in the Danehill Parish Historical Society magazine, was a mine of information; The East Sussex Records Office for many documents from the Sheffield Park archives; 98-year-old Roy Lingham who shared his invaluable memories of life at The Sheffield Arms from 1934 to 2000; Roger Packham, who allowed me to use illustrations and texts from his excellent book: Cricket in the Park, The Life and Times of Lord Sheffield 1832 to 1909; Jill Rolfe for tracking down many old photographs of the Sheffield Arms, and to Peter Richardson for allowing me to use some from his collection. Thanks, too, to Peter Wigan for lending the photograph of the Australian cricket team.

I'm grateful to Tom Reeves, for the photograph of the 1942 Home Guards' Christmas party at the Sheffield Arms taken by his father, then Private Edward Reeves.

I'd like to thank those who also gave me their personal memories of the Sheffield Arms: Edith Wood and Maurice Forbes-Wood, John Howe, Philip Gregory, Julian Foreman, Barbara Johnson, Kristan Fawcus; and Andrew Hudson for permission to use his Fletching Village Voice stories from the Sussex Express.

I very much appreciated help from Carola Symington who lent me useful books about the local area; Jim Spencer and Fiona Flower who put me in touch with people who had their own memories of the Sheffield Arms; Carole Thornton, Elizabeth Sargent and Nichola Schulz for suggesting local contacts; and Mary Butterfield for permission to use articles from the Fletching Parish magazine.

My thanks to Jeremy Alexander, Chris Whittick and Mark Wigglesworth for their very useful proof reading, to Andy Gammon for the care and skill he brought to designing the book, and to Chris Wigglesworth for his always cheering support. A particular thank you to Tony Tree for his invaluable help with the photographs.

Flower illustrations
Angelica, page 21
Meadow Sweet, page 33
Fennel, page 38
Chamomile, inside back cover

Front cover:
The Sheffield Arms c1830.
Photo by kind permission of Trading Boundaries.